# TOXIC HOPE

*in between heartbreaks*

## JELETTA JOSE

BookLeaf
Publishing

India | USA | UK

Made with ❤ on the BookLeaf Publishing Platform
www.bookleafpub.in
www.bookleafpub.com

# Dedication

To IAN—
You are the light in my darkest moments, the reason I rise, and the heart of every dream I chase. May you always know the strength of your own story.

To the one who stands beside me—
Your love is my refuge, your presence my peace. Thank you for believing in me when I forget to believe in myself.

And to the dreamers, the broken, the mended, and the ones still finding their way—
These words are for you. May you never stop seeking, never stop feeling, and never stop writing your own story.

# Preface

You live, you die...
You breakdown. You cry.
You shatter your heart and trash your soul,
into a million tears.
yet you try!

Let the world not pry,
show only what's visible to
those wandering eyes!

As cliched as it may seem,
Reading these lines might feel futile.
But pray, do hang on...
It will be worth your while.

# Acknowledgements

This book is a piece of my heart, a collection of moments that shaped me, broke me, and rebuilt me. It would not have been possible without the love, lessons, and losses that inspired these words.

To the one who stands beside me now—thank you for showing me that love doesn't have to hurt. Your patience, understanding, and unwavering belief in me have given me the courage to share these words with the world.

To those who left, only to return too late—thank you for the heartbreaks and the lessons. Without you, this book wouldn't exist.

To my readers—If you have ever loved the wrong person, struggled to move on, or found yourself in the wreckage of something that once felt right, this book is for you. Thank you for picking it up, for seeing yourself in these pages, and for allowing my words to be part of your journey.

And finally, to the version of me who thought she wouldn't survive—you did. And now, your words live on.

# 1. Done!

And today
when I wanted to write
About all those years.
The wasted tears,
Traumatised & Oppressed,
Ages of verbal demeaning long speeches,
Body & soul caged for ages.
Every form of tyranny at hand,
never-ending toxicity of a span.

.

I couldn't...

.

I'd no more words,
No more thoughts.

.

To impart for your deceitful self,
Though the images flashed in my head,
Constant.
My two cents for you.
Well,
It was done!

# 2. And then...

It isn't easy... It isn't hard.
It's just... what it is!
You could do anything and everything
To keep yourself absorbed,
to not let your mind wander off
To just be...

And yet... there you are
Struggling to get rid of those
invisible weights,
Gasping to breath.
begging the inevitable
to flee...
Working your way through
with your mask on.
With a smile pasted
Right on.

You thought that the demons
were night crawlers, (Yeah?)
you'd thought their visit would be limited
Like in the stories?
Haa... (what a fool you've been.)
They live & breed within you,

Your worries feed 'em
Your peace repels 'em
And they aren't scared off easily
in this constant tug of war
Each day passes off to another
Some days you win,
And then some.

# 3. Ticking Clock

I don't have forever.
All I get is the time between now and the final goodbye.
How can I love you
Knowing the same
That I don't have the time!
That the freaking time bomb
can blast at any point...
And the scar will rue for me to cherish
For you're and always will be my favourite 'If only'...
But how can I not love you knowing that everything I
ever wanted,
Every dream I ever had,
Is just right there in front of me...
And I just hopelessly fell for it.
Knowing the aftermath well,
Knowing that this might be it.
The final quintessence of this
Hopelessly beating heart.

# 4. Bibliophagist

Turning the pages, it felt alive
His smile, his eyes shining on mine,
His fingers lingering over my skin,
Demanding that craving sensation
from each of the tiny cells in my being.
A glimpse of his face,
and it would all stop,
Lord knows, I'd tried to fix my eyes on that page.

If only!

Love was lurking around in the air.
Any resistance seemed bizarre.
Its soft wind breezing over the pages,
tugged along the little fat plumpy boy,
wearing his mischievous smile,
Winking at the space between us.
Struck with the inevitable,
Stuck within the lines,
reading in between,
for a possible out, to the sane world.
Lord knows,
I'd tried to fix my eyes between those lines...

If only!

Another page, closing the proximity
'tween two souls.
His breath on my neck, sending goosebumps all over,
The scent of his body wash and after shave,
filling in the air.
One more page, and I'll be doomed,
Lord knows, I'd tried to fix myself on that page.

If only!

A vibrating smart phone,
sending multiple shivers down my spine,
Your sculpted face flashing on the screen...
few seconds to realization,
(Damn!! Damn!!)
A second too f**king late,
Now all the possible lovers
(the good and the bad ones)
on every piece I'll ever read,
had to have a resemblance to you.

Lord knows, I tried.
Lord knows, my plight
And now I'll have to endure the wait...
till it's demise.

If Only!

# 5. You

Every Now and Then,
You slither in to my long
lost unending chain of thoughts,
and declare your reign for
the longest while.
Oh... what I didn't do to get
you out of there.
What all I tried, to
shut my mind off that trail.
The more I tried,
the worse it got.
For You'd your claim,
and this astray heart was,
the one to be blamed!

I knew, you thought
you were unreachable
and the distance only adding up to it.
But, my dear, you were not
unattainable,
not even if you'd wished!
That tough, reckless exterior,
had to have a Heart
pretending to be of stone,

which I, for all my reasons, sought.
And somewhere across the time,
was I hoping to find my quest?
quench my thirst,
and claim what's mine?

# 6. Thoughts I cannot fathom!

Listening to the soft rush of leaves,
As the branches moved, along with the breeze
With every passing Tik-Tok of the second hand,
Memories flood in, of all the time
that had passed by.
A lot to regret,
A lot to surpass,
A lifetime worth of questions,
Never a moment to ask.
Many lanes did I pass by,
In the never-ending quest to find me
Facing a dead alley at every turn,
Finding myself a step away from the big jump,
The edges narrowed with every run.
A pause, a please, a thought
That was always at stake—to burn.

With every passing Tik-Tok of the second hand,
A mystery waited to be unraveled,
Every page of the yearbook
Rendered and read.
The joy of the time that passed by,
Of all the memories which wouldn't die,

About how you made a difference,
And worse, you couldn't deny!

With every passing tik-tok of the second hand,
The minute's hand accompanied, Every once in a while.
The journey to find the labyrinth wasn't tranquil.
Until I was steered by you to realize
It was 'straight and fast',
As it always has been.
All the dubiousness of how it was going to be,
Effaced itself and left no place for ambiguity.
Your presence was all it required.
But what would it take from me to be sired?

With every Tik-Tok, minutes passed into long hours,
The quest to Neverland is on a spree.
Discovering a new sense of something,
which wasn't there to be!
With you, every moment felt infinite.
For in your arms, it was meant to be
Intrepid, ravishing, arbitrary.
This life may cease,
For time can't be pleased, but
with You, I'll be at ease,
**"For I may not have forever,
But I do have... "**

# 7. If Only

It seems right...
It feels so right, at times!
though I'm still occupied in the daze...
It doesn't seem real anymore!
Your thoughts linger on my mind,
they just wander around,
but never seems to leave!

The night is sly and young...
I've been drowsy for so long,
so much that it refuses to go on.
You would creep onto the bed, and
hold me with that urge,
to savour every moment of this,
It seems as unreal to you as to me.
To be there and be lost in each other's eyes,
and to see the magic crawl in with every touch.
Real or not, I held you close...
wrapped around my fingers.
I could feel your fingertips wandering all over me,
exploring and claiming your reach...
dipping into the moment,
like a boy, drenched and lost in the rain,
still unable to quench his thirst...

with every passing moment, asking for more.
That one touch was enough to wake my soul,
to perceive you as mine,
your hands around me, searching for a place to rest.
our lips lost in admiration, wandering in
soft, sensuous, and wild
kisses everywhere...
breathless and snogging,
Your lips left mine in a rush
trembling for more, my eyes opened
in a haste and hush!
There you were, gazing at me,
searching for something, in the depth of my eyes,
A smile spread over the corner of your lips
and you found your way towards me,
all I could do was blush and turn
scarlet red... beaming with radiance
and sinking down with excitement.
Your lips found their way through...
compelling me to ask for more,
more of you... much more of it.
I could sense your lips widening into a mischievous grin,
for you knew my body so well.
With a swift wrench, it crumpled at your mercy.
I was there with you,
Before losing my senses.

A sudden tug at the back of my neck
where your fingers were drawing circles
a moment ago, forced me to look around
Only to find myself alone...
utterly amazed to see you gone,
I sat there, drifting my thoughts to hunt
for a cue,
to grasp what was going on.

But there you were,
entering through the door,
with those saucy eyes, telling me
that you missed me more,
hoping on to bed,
with a peck on my forehead,
to tell me about your day...
unable to hide the daze,
searching for the right words to say,
still flushed and beaming,
I turned to face you, to admire that face,
to see that smile, to look into those eyes...
which always seem to search for answers in mine!
Slowly, your hands reached to caress my cheeks...
and my lips found yours just in time,
before I could silently scream,
that I couldn't miss you
even in my wildest dreams.

# 8. Where do I stand?

Would you miss me when I'm not around?
Would you miss me when I'm gone?
When my head says, you won't
my heart wants to believe otherwise
and go on!

You won't be mine,
I won't be yours.
My once upon a time
reaches ashore...
We would be strangers
to the rest of the world
yet again!

Sure, my head does know the best
but this stupid heart goes on,
'focus on now, and f**k the rest !! '
you clearly made your choice,
and definitely left me out alone.
I was never supposed to be in it.
was I?

I couldn't figure out what this is.
or what it was between us?

Or maybe it was just me.
blindly falling into the pit.
Because for you...
I was maybe yet another glitch.
But for me...
That glitch created the biggest stitch.

# 9. Always!

I always knew.
that forever doesn't exist
cause it never did.
Still taking the risk seemed irrefutable
knowing that,
I won't be looking at you like this,
you won't be looking at me,
the way you do now.
We won't be walking together, side by side.
softly brushing the skin,
Our fingers entwined.
I won't be playing with your hair,
we won't be looking into each other's eyes,
kissing like there's no end to it,
like it's the end of the world.
I won't be the one to wake next to you in the morning.
I no longer will be the reason for those few moments
when your eyes sparkled like a child,
or will I be??
Guess I'll never know.

I knew... always did.
Forever is a lie; who doesn't know that!
You can never have anything,

Forever.
All you get is now,
for what happens afterwards
Is never what you really want.

# 10. HIM

I let her go.
She was getting attached
a lot...
She was too good for me.

I let her go.
She was being caring
a lot...
I felt so restricted
I couldn't fly!

I let her go.
We'd no future.
She doesn't rely on me for anything.
I don't feel needed here at all.
I found another
in no time!
This will destroy her
Trust in men... forever.

I let her go
and kept her
at the same time.
This will make her

hate herself more
and question her own worth
every time.

# 11. HER

I think I love him.
I can't imagine a moment without him.
He's always on my mind.

I think I love him,
but I shouldn't... haven't I been here before?
What if it ends the same way?
What if I'm left alone?
Again... in pieces?
Maybe this time will be different.

I think I love him.
He's mine to take care of.
I'll give him all my love,
which I never got in my life!

I think I love him.
But he's aloof these days.
He's ignoring me,
Spending less time with me.

I think I love him.
But he's away all the time.
We barely talk now.

Even while lying next to him,
he seems way too far away.

I think I love him
But I guess there's someone else now.
It looks like I wasn't enough.
I didn't keep him happy.
He's found it somewhere else!
But what did I do wrong?
How can I bring him back?
Why am I never enough?
Why does this keep happening to me?

I think I love him.
But he's in love with another!

# 12. Reminiscence

It's easy to fake a smile,
When you know it's all a lie!
It's easy to blame time,
When you knew all along
you were the one acting blind!
Its damn easy to pretend
To be fine, to show that it's not killing you,
To see that you're not the only one,
To be more precise... you were never the one!

It's always easy to pretend when you're in love,
Closing your eyes and ears to reality.
And much easier to
Pick up the pieces, after
He leaves for another, his 'one'!
It's easier to pretend that you are okay,
When you died a million times,
And still do, thinking of the times.
Hoping it never ended...
wishing it never happened.

It's always easy to pretend...
When you love someone and they don't,
To pretend that someday they just might...

till you realise, for them
you won't suffice!

# 13. Promise?

If the chances in this life
tends to shorten it's while,
Inch by inch
with every approaching sting.
Remember I'd still Love you,
Love to know you,
More and in a better way.
Love to be with you.
(Call me crazy,
I don't see a reason why not, though!)

I'll always love you...
(Believe It. period.)

I don't want it to be left,
As an unfinished story for later,
Course, there won't be a 'later'.
Duh!!

Let's make it worthwhile,
and not create a Void,
to look back upon,
As long as we share it
Let's dwell on it...

Even after taking all the trouble,
If it's not meant to be, this time.
(obviously Timing can be a REAL B*tch, as always!)

Pray, do Promise me the next,
and the next after that, and beyond.
Cause I won't be done...
Nor then or ever, with you.
Or maybe not for the longest while ever possible,
For that's how long I would love to be with you,
the more, the better!
But hey! that's all about me,
and how bad I've got it (stupid me!)

So, here is the deal,
Please help me make it real...
If not this lifetime,
As the chances seems thin
Pray, do Promise me
The next seven/nine...
(whatever the number it is)
Even if it's by default,
Be mine!

# 14. Never

Never meant to fall in Love,
never meant to be together,
Destiny brought them near
kept them close to each other.
"I love you a lot," she whispered.
gazing at the deep, dark, pouring sky,
as the night shared her hushed cry...

The sky was starless.
while all she looked up was for one,
Night after night they met,
talked for hours at a stretch,
he never got tired of her pouring out her heart,
She'd found a good listener, at last.
All he did was smile through his starlit eyes,
without shifting his gaze in any plight.
She beamed in his presence,
like a thousand stars burning bright,
blushed when she caught him,
looking at her, *like he only had eyes for her.*

As the night bonded so well,
with her lonesome self,
they called on for the 'one.'

the one who never really left,
the one who has always kept apace
with her ever-changing spirit.
and was still missed.

This night,
even as the crowd passed by
her gaze kept rooted on
the unattainable sky.
For she knew,
somewhere in the same moonlit sky,
he'll be watching her, close by
with that heart stopping smile
And for that only,
She knew she'd fake her smile.
Hide her over brimming eyes,
and live on...
pretending as if he never died.

# 15. Guilty

When Hope is all, you have...
Would you look back?
When you know the answers
Would it please to question again?
Love... a known Evol, unknown to all
sent to this world, a torment to befall.
Love, they say, is never jealous.
Yet that is all you get!

To love you was never my plan.
yet to love you was my destiny.
You were a lesson and a blessing,
Still, were you everything?

First time, they say is sweet!
What they don't know is that it is always sweet.
And was it wise to shatter all of it?
in a glance, for another?

This scar is your gift to me.
I will treasure it,
It is my precious, I'll to hold onto it.
To love you was my desire,
and to behold it in this life is my pain!

A sweet tormenting reminder,
for the rest of the ages that I might live.

Love, they say, happens once
Only once in a lifetime its true!
But what if I've loved again?
Will it not be wise?
Will it not be true to me??
To love again. Scares me...
just a mere thought is enough
to bury my soul back to its
cradling grave.
I shall not love again.
the shattered pieces shall
Join, in vain!

# 16. Who Knew

Has it been few months,
or weeks or days...
I couldn't say,
still feels like yesterday.
Like those,
Missing pieces of broken clay.
Yet to be found,
Yet to be known.

It was some
hasty movement of hands,
a turning touch and snap!
Downwards it fell,
Crushed like gel,
Broken and vanished
into various unknown spells.

Still lost,
somewhere in that
pit of darkness.
Still stubborn to let anyone in...
And be found.
Still hiding from those hands
To be touched again,

And be known
And recovered.

It was just to know
The way,
The way that leads to you.
You only had to let me in,
And let me know
What dwells inside of you...
Though lost in transcription
yet wondering,
It didn't feel like a different addiction.
Still a train wreck,
still a risk,
yet I was ready for that
Voyage with you.
Going after the mist of aloofness,
Wandering Into the depths
of that hard exterior,
To reach the 'Unreachable' you.

You only had to let me in
And make it known
For who knew
It would have been a perfect fit.
It would have grown

Together
Than fall apart.

# 17. Blurred

There is an Obvious response
in every unspoken word,
in every blank expression,
in every sigh and prolonged
pause...

For every ramble,
every voice muttering inside the mind
contrasting every right and wrong.
counting all the regrets,
all the DO's and DON'T's
sweeping blames on all the missed
chances and come backs,
There is always an obvious response.
Never to be heard,
ever to be told!

Blinded by the mirage of joy,
by the 'oh...' moments,
by the daydreaming,
which was nothing else
but nightmares in disguise...
wishing to know
this from that,

wish if only I'd known
these countless disasters in life.

35

For every Damn thing,
There is always an obvious response!

# 18. Reverie

Last night I saw you,
I know it's not possible.
but I did.
I saw you so many times,
laughing, smiling,
pondering, irritated, angry...
I saw all of it.

Were all those emotions for me?
I'll know not!
For you were not alone,
rather we weren't.
The known unknown
stranger to me and
a person for you,
chaperoned like your shadow.

No, it wasn't a mere figment.
I wasn't overdoing it.
I didn't make it up!
It was just a dream
or a series of them,
seen and rued.

It was mine, though
It didn't feel so, anyhow!
Was I gazing into the
alternative?
The parallel, where
the lies and reasons
were all out, and yet
It looked happy.

Maybe that would have been your life.
if I hadn't meddled in on it.
maybe it was your happily ever ... whatever
had I not been there.
Maybe it still is.
and am just in the grey!

To-night...
My head aches,
my eyelids close on the shutter
but I'm scared to close my eyes,
and fall into the abyss.
scared I might dream again,
dreams of you.

# 19. Sting

It started to crawl in,
slowly...
making its way under my skin
reaching for the unknown.
Every movement it made,
I could feel an inch of me.
dying within,
crying and trembling,
withering away in pain,
with every single moment.
I could feel every bit inside of me.
crumpling, yearning for a little more,
pleading a second further...
As it started to rise,
to achieve the desired,
turning a deaf ear to my sobs,
putting up a set of blind eyes to my tears,
Every second,
it invaded what was mine,
mine to be,
claimed its reign
and forbidding
any other reach!
This pain felt fresh.

though it wasn't new in anyway,
different from the rest.

As the cries became louder,
It felt hollow inside.
the words could not
reach up to your eardrums,
or to mine.
But you were not there,
no one was,
Was I doomed with this forever?
Left alone to shout and scream,
curse aloud, in vain.
It only took the stretch to realize,
I couldn't hear my own cry,
It was lost in the baffled state,
while I could see myself,
lying down on the floor,
crushing my knees to my chest,
motionless...
I felt transcended.
from this life to the other,
only to feel the agony,
up till this elevated level!
It didn't take much time to realize it.
Yeah!! I was going to make it.
Period.

This is it,
the moment I longed for.
Did he really hear my plea after all?
I'd be happy at last,
but forlorn I felt!
Even at this hour.

I felt this urge,
to tell you all of this,
all about it,
about how it felt,
about how it feels,
to feel that it is near.
Yet even then
the cynicism prevailed,
't wouldn't matter,
't wouldn't satisfy,
then why would I long for this?
Did the Devil take my memory with his?
Knowing the required retort already,
I couldn't die yet.
Hell! I wasn't ready.

# 20. Could I?

I loved you; I really did.
I still love you,
and I'll always do.


Every night, lying awake throughout,
I wondered to myself,
Why do I still hang on to you?
You are gone...
only this silence is left
to trail the path between us.
You were gone,
for good or bad?
I couldn't possibly tell.
but it was Your decision,
So, it had to be for your good.
Why do I still hold on to the memories?
to those echoes of the past,
which made me giggle with excitement.
which made me blush,
I got fixated on your words.
for they are lodged in my mind,
showing this side of yours,
which wanted me... wanted us.
You were gone,

and I was left to mourn,
Should I or not?
either way, I couldn't go on.
Somewhere I was happy,
Happy that you got out of the mess,
got out of any further complications...
Happy that somewhere,
You were happy!
Feeling sad wasn't an option,
it was inevitable.
cause I loved you...
I'd feel bad.
But this muteness only made me
feel worse...
Your words would have
given a sense to this episode,
but the tranquillity could only magnify
the terrible tale of internal misery!
You were gone
and I could only brood about you.
you,
you and
just YOU!
Call me crazy, but that's all I did.
all I could do!
Time called for answers,
but to kill it, I could only obsess

about You!
Making up various scenarios in my mind,
of what I would say if we ever talked,
what I would do if we ever met,
and what not.

I played it all out
in my mind,
time and time again.
Till I knew what made it possible,
What made you go?
I knew somehow, I played a part in it.
I knew; now I had to stop.
God!
If I could ever do that.
You were gone, and
I could understand why.
Believe it or not,
But I did try.
I could reason out the contradictions,
between your words and deeds...
I could sort and intercede.
I could totally agree with
Since you were gone
and I was freed!

# 21. Let Go

Were You Really Lost?
within your own?
being alone all by yourself
running away from every memory,
that could possibly remind you
of that time. Thinking
it was the right step to take.
**was it**???
Why couldn't you just say it?
say it out loud that you were being
choked in it, gasping for air.
You found no other way out!
saying all this might have helped you
with your trouble, eased your pain
for who was going to stop you,
stop you from running and
hiding?
Not **me!!**


*My Luv, My Dear...*
you weren't alone in that maze,
somewhere at a distance was I, lost in a daze.
Trying to figure it out,

trying to break loose,
trying to make sense of it all,
at least for once, before
giving it up completely.
But why was it called Love again?
Why, I couldn't possibly get an answer to that!
Why?
When you were being compromised,
where you'd no voice,
where all you ever wanted was to flee.
Yet this half-wit heart
could never break free
of those chains,
for somehow, even after all this
I still believed you had its key.

Don't be so lost, my love.
maybe our journey was only
this short...
yet to smother in it
was not a plausible thought.
all we ever had to do
was to open up
and yet,
after all that while,
We had lost that touch!

Don't **hate me,**
for I don't **hate you.**
because this is for the best,
and you do know the rest.

# 22. Let it be

Let it be like this.
staying away from everything,
everything that might take it away.
Accepting reality as it is,
maybe it is meant to be,
or not.
Whatever it is, let's keep **mum.**

Life is not fair. It never is!
It doesn't come around
the way you want it to be;
yet somehow you carry on living,
hoping that someday it might...
*It just might...!*

My **love**, My **life**,
nothing goes accordingly.
for anybody.
Neither will it ever change,
for any possible reason
people could ever give.
Either be my **Miracle** or do it for me!
Until then, do not *mortify* me

for living my life... my way,
Let me be!

# 23. Fate

I still fear the inevitable.
I still dream about it.
It might not be my fate
Yet I can't stop how it feels.
You gave me resilience
when I was fragile,
but that strength drains off.
I can't hold it tight.

I believed in you,
since I knew I couldn't believe in me.
I wanted you to be the pillar of my strength,
the strength that you gave me.
Yet I couldn't show it to you...
and it wasn't enough to be true.

All of my fears have come true,
but I couldn't complain.
cause, so often do my dreams.
Dreams I could not dwell upon,
for the fear of that old wound,
left a fresh scar... every time!

Trust me, I fell apart with every stab...

yet I stood there trying to hold it together.
I don't know if I can do it again,
for what it takes... lacks in me!
But if fate decides to play,
I'll still be there with a smile on the brim.

# 24. HIM: Fumbled Love

She's glowing...
in that pale green saree
with those rosy cheeks
in lovely glee.
Her head tilted to a side,
eyes wide... searching
for something or someone
in the crowd... with pride.
The long dangling pearls,
brushing her soft neck.
Her lips... slightly parted and raw,
capturing those twinkling eyes in all it's awe!

I could go on... about every bit of her.
If only I could look away
from this endless stare...

My fingers kept tracing her jaws,
the plump of her lips...
recalling every bit of how
it felt on my skin.

My heart kept longing
for her...

to see her like this,
her smile,
that gaze, which followed me for a while.
To see her move with that elegance and grace...
to see her in every way
was my only HIGH!

I kept tracing my fingers
along her cheeks,
all I could do was
stare and have my fill.
For the screen would
never compare to her skin,
but it was all I had left
to calm my beating
heart and blame my selfish act.

# 25. Memories

Her fingernails left a mark
on me...
Her words were magic to
my soul...
Her smile melted something
in my heart...
Her touch healed wounds
within.

Her presence made all
the difference,
It lifted my spirit.
a boost possibly seen.

Her eyes traced my face,
searched something
deep in my eyes.
It asked so many queries,
had so many qualms.
Had she known what it did to me,
I'm definite; she would have stopped!

She walked beside me,
our fingers slightly touched,

Jitters of hope rushed
down my spine.
I was just hoping for
our stars to align!

She stood there,
next to me...
our shoulders brushed ,
she was talking to someone
nonchalant, at her best.
Had she known what it was doing to me,
I'm definite; she would rest!

She was mine,
(was I thine?)
It was a blissful time,
more for me,
cause I shine!
Her radiance worked on me.
I could go to the moon
and back on time.
She gave away so much.
Sometimes, I felt her divine!

My heart was beating
but I was in charge,
I was feeling things

and I knew it wasn't fine.

Her life was a rollercoaster
and if it was any way around
I'd have been bolder.

I can't catch feelings
It'll get me off my game,
I can't turn vulnerable
I don't think I'll give
her, my surname --

Though she is perfect
for me,
But maybe I'll get
a better chance.
I need to withdraw
and let her keep hanging
by the straw.

Months passed by
I think I found the
ideal option,
only to figure out later,
that in neglecting her chaos...
and going after the "alleged"
perfection,

I was being blind,
living in DELUSION!

# 26. HER: Unrequited Love



It's been months,
since he left me
to pick up my shattered self.

For someone who
was in pieces for years,
He was my peace,
for a brief period!

I cried, I mourned
tried to level up
the toxicity in my life,
with intoxication of my soul.

Every second felt like
a leap year...
the memories creeping in,
all the while, turned
into a constant fear!

A whole lot of
tarot reading and
manifestation reels later,
I found my strength again,

only self-love, mental health,
and self-worth to regain!

Dressing up, listening to those songs again.
Going out, meeting others,
posting on socials,
changing pictures....
Life felt normal,
for a change!

But the ritual of
searching for those eyes in the crowd
didn't seem to fail.

I know he denied me,
and most definitely
despises me...
and I've made my peace with it!
I know he will never think of me,
like I do...
That is how it should be!

But would he be familiar,
if we ever come across?
I'm sure he's got a better one to look at now.
Would he ever recall
the intimacy?

I'm sure it would have surpassed
from history!

We will be known strangers
to the world,
one overburdened with memories
other... free from it!

In the end, what remains is
the Ugly Truth, that
is going to rue.
The pattern repeats itself,
and even...
This one couldn't be TRUE.

# 27. Hurt?

Does it hurt, still?
Yes, it does.
How much, though?

Oh, if words
could describe the pain I go through...
It hurts so much
that I can watch him,
Living my future with her...
right in front of my eyes,
and not be bittersweet about it!
Even if it kills every cell
in my being...
I'll still be thrilled
and pretend to be well.

# 28. Dishevelled

There's Black, there's White
Yet I'm thrown into the Grey...

There's Right, there's Wrong
Still, I'm perplexed by the known...

There's Good, there's Evil
But I'm always waiting at the tip of
the double-edged sword...

There's Happy, there's Sad
And I'm drowning in the pit of numbness...

There's Heaven, there's Hell
Though I'm forever stuck in the Netherworld.

# 29. Triger Warning

If you see an anxious person,
Would you recognize?
If you see a soul dealing with depression,
Would you sympathize?

Or
Would you wait for them to sob?
scream, be breathless,
faint or look like a ghost of a person?

Yeah...
I know you would!
The world works in such ways...
Every condition has a prerequisite.
Check box to be filled
And if you don't fit into those boxes...
You're just asking for attention, B*tc*!

So
If the person looks like this.
Happy... sober... living the life... and all the whatnots!
With all the smiles and laughs,
What would you think?
Would you fathom the grief within?

Naahh...
Unless you see them begging on their knees
with bloodshot eyes digging into their skull...
Nobody will know!

But hey...
Anyone going through it would know.
We don't look it.
Like how the societal norms term it to be.

But
Most of the time...
We just look like this!
For all the upheavals inside,
We'll be in our best disguise!

# 30. Masquerade

It looks easy
It looks amazing
It looks like you've got everything under control.
It does, doesn't it?

And for everyone else,
Sometimes...You pretend.
You wear a mask for the world
(all the... f**king time)
Cause they would never really get you,
For 'em... everything is perfect in their world.
So are you!!! Really?

And that mask—the pretentious one,
That comes up every time I'm not alone.
It covers up the thoughts I get.
It fucking doesn't let the eyes shower.
It puts out a better version of me, more than I ever
could...

Hell, it is ME!!!
So much so that it doesn't ever come off. its always there.
Even when it becomes
Difficult to smile

Difficult to pretend
Difficult to cry
Difficult to breathe
Difficult to LIVE.

# 31. Adieu!

To my world, which shattered
right in front of me...
to the mirage of the prefect one, which revealed
the ugly truth of pretence,
to the sweet-malicious words,
with no comparisons,
to all the false hopes of trust
and faith,
to my Hazel-eyed version
of love and woe...
**Adieu!!**

# 32. Unveiled

The Happiest Day of her Life,
Dressed in the blessed Scarlet Red,
Adorned with precious jewels,
Crimson-red designs of 'mehendi'
reaching up onto her elbows and knees,
like printed on a mosaic.
A tinted layer of bloody red
hiding her perfectly crafted, beautiful face,
shielding the rueful 'kajal' eyes,
while the prying watchers, sigh!!

Eyes that'd dreamed of this day,
This one day and hence after,
on many sleepless nights.
The day when she'll be the happiest
one on this earth,
Twirling and giggling
in her newly made gown,
Flaunting it with glee to one and all.
Trying on the trinkets,
Putting on everything to gaze
at the marvel 't all could do
to her glittering eyes and blushing cheeks,
cherry dew lips... brimming with

a mischievous smile.
Adorned like a Princess,
She couldn't wait to be His Queen.
forever and on,
For a happy life with a fairy tale ending.
waiting to see the expression on His face,
When she'd walk up to the pedestal... priceless!!!

A lifetime worth of joy,
Glistening in her eyes.
Memories pouring down the old lane,
as she sat there staring at
The Vermilion, for having it
she had to pay the price,
all the dreams of Love die, with
its first pinch, kissing her forehead.
She sat there, shielded from all the cries.
The promise, honoured, while she tries...

A True Princess, a soulful Daughter,
Walking up to the 'mandap'
with her parents on either side,
Oh! What she wouldn't have done,
to see them beaming like this!
Their eyes filled with pride.
As of now, without any lies,
blessing her in all abundance.

As she raised her eyes to where he stood,
Hoping to console her beating heart,
That she could do this.
as she knew what she wished for,
Wouldn't be found, but
while she looked at his gloating face,
Time dragged its way,
and every second was like an hour at bay.
With every step she took towards him,
His eyes fixed on her.
Smiling with joy,
A small boy who got his favourite pony,
Dearly precious, even to let 'it out of sight.
 Two twinkling stars made a silent Promise,
***"Forever and hence!"***
And she knew, "**She'll *be loved!***"

# 33. Meant to be

The tears dazzling
 in her eyes...
words choking her voice
a compelled curve
of a faint smile,
reminding the rue of
the final goodbye.
With an imprint of
memories in her heart
she watched him
walk... past her,
down the aisle.

www.ingramcontent.com/pod-product-compliance
Lightning Source LLC
LaVergne TN
LVHW010020200726
843495LV00015B/1840